BYGONE SWINDON

Frontispiece: The crest of the Municipal Borough of Swindon. This was granted by Queen Victoria by a Charter of Incorporation on 22 January 1900. The four quarters represent both old and new Swindon. The winged wheel represents swift railway travel. The mitre represents Odo, Bishop of Bayeux, to whom William the Conqueror gave Swindon in 1066. The three crescents symbolise the Goddard family, and the three castles symbolise the Vilett family, landowners in New Swindon. The motto means 'Health and Industry', and this is shown pictorially by the strong arm holding the crossed hammers at the top.

Bygone SWINDON

Michael A. Howell

Michael A. Howell
12th December 1984.

Phillimore

1984

Published by
PHILLIMORE & CO. LTD.
Shopwyke Hall, Chichester, Sussex

© The Swindon Society, 1984

ISBN 0 85033 538 8

Printed and bound in Great Britain by
BILLING & SONS LTD
Worcester, England

LIST OF ILLUSTRATIONS

To the people of the
railway town of Swindon

ACKNOWLEDGEMENTS

The author would like to thank Denis Bird and the Swindon Society for the use of photographs from their collections, also the researchers of the Swindon Society: Carole New, Mike Brougham, Tony Daglish, Roger Trayhurn, Brian Bridgeman, David Luker, and Joan Jefferies.

The author would also like to give very special thanks to Christopher L. Scott and Pamela Golding. Thanks are also extended to Mrs. F. M. Scott whose memories are incorporated in the introduction to this book.

Other people and organisations who have helped greatly with the compilation of this book are: Wiltshire Newspapers, Wiltshire Library and Museum Services, British Rail (Western Region), Mr. M. Fox, Mr. G. E. Lait, Miss K. Cook, the Oxford Publishing Company, Mr. G. Wirdnam, the Rev. Canon W. J. Cratchley, Ridgeway Studios, and Raychem, to whom the author extends grateful thanks.

INTRODUCTION

'The hill upon which pigs live' is hardly a glamorous name for a town, but it reflects the town's function as a livestock market for many centuries. We know that there was a market in Swindon in 1274, although it is likely that markets had been taking place perhaps 15 years previously. As late as 1626 Charles I granted Thomas Goddard the right to hold a market once a week on a Monday in Swindon, as well as the right to hold two fairs or feasts yearly, one on the second Monday in May and the other on the second Monday in December. Goddard would have been able to charge stallholders at these events a rental for the right to erect a stall, and would also have taken a proportion of the profits made.

A map of 1773 shows Swindon very much as it had been at the time of the Domesday Survey in 1086, still a typical Wiltshire market town built round four main streets. Wood Street was formerly known as Windmill Street; a windmill, on the site of the present *King's Arms Hotel*, was certainly there in 1324. Later it was also known as Blacksmith Street, as two forges were sited there. Devizes Road was the location for the early horse fairs, the remainder of the market's business being carried on in the Square. As it was lined by two hawthorn hedges, this street was known as 'Short Hedge'. The High Street has always been so called, but Newport Street was formerly known as 'Bull Street' after the public house of that name, which can itself be traced back to 1346.

The Market Square has long since lost its 17th-century cross and stocks. From the 15th to the 19th centuries, Wiltshire wool had a reputation second to none in Europe, and Swindon, being so close to the Wiltshire Downs, excellent sheep country, was the ideal location for many refugee Dutch and Flemish weavers to establish themselves. It is said to have been their partiality to Holland's gin which started the smuggling trade in Swindon. Barrels of spirits were landed on the Hampshire coast, and brought to the town at night by ancient pathways over the downs. The smuggling network worked like clockwork for over two hundred years. Beneath the streets of the Old Town is a whole network of tunnels which were used for moving the contraband secretly about Swindon. Many of them lead to the manor house called 'The Lawn'.

The cellars beneath the present Town Hall were important in the smuggling trade, providing a well-known hiding place. Gravestones form the steps down to the cellars where, the story goes, the ghost of Lawrence, once head cellarman, still haunts the vaults.

The Square was the setting for the last bout of 'Backswording', a violent game which was played upon a wide stage about 7 feet high and 14 or 15 feet long by 10 or 12 feet wide. It was usually erected where the *Rifleman's Arms* now stands. Players were given a piece of linen tape, the ends of which were sewn together. This tape was placed around the left thigh and also around the thumb of the left hand, which had the effect of preventing the wearer raising his left arm beyond a horizontal position about level with the top of his head. Players then made a selection from a number of ash sticks about 3 or 4 feet long, one end of which was covered with a small basket as a protection for the hand. The object of each player was to protect his head from his opponent's stick whilst trying to strike the other man and make blood flow.

Bull baiting was carried on in the Square until about 1810 or 1812. The pole to which the bull was chained was a large oaken post let into a socket or square frame of timber. When the first drainage works were being carried out, this frame was dug up from the course of the drain from Dammas Lane into the High Street.

As well as being a market centre, Swindon was essentially a limestone town: quarries have been worked here for over three centuries. A quality Purbeck limestone was produced which, as well as being used extensively in local construction work, was used to repave London after the Great Fire in 1666.

After the formation of the Swindon Market Company in the mid-19th century, old stables and warehouses in the Square were pulled down and the Market House – later known as the Town Hall – erected on the site. In 1852 the cellars were let to Messrs. Brown and Nephew for wine stores. The Corn Exchange was erected and opened in 1866. The Swindon post office was originally sited at the *Bell Hotel*; a portion of one bar was set apart for mail, which was dealt with by the barmaid, the boots and the waiter.

All the streets of Old Swindon have their own points of interest: *Cricklade Street* was the start of the old coach road to Cricklade. The gradient was formerly much more severe, as it originally ran at the same height as the raised stone footpath. It was already known by its present name in 1663, and a century later we know that it was lined with trees. One house, 'Townsends' (1729), was previously known as 'The Hall'. Its earliest known occupant was a Mr. Harding, to whose memory a tablet was erected in the parish church, still to be seen today. When the stocks were removed from the Square, they were placed opposite the church here. The bank on the corner of Wood Street and Cricklade Street first opened its doors on Thursday 5 February 1885.

Dammas Lane led to the damson orchard of 'The Lawn'. The first reference to this lane occurred in 1684, though the name is certainly older. The spelling has varied over the years.

The name *Devizes Road* first occurs in a *Loyal Almanac* published in 1858, when the earliest houses were built there. As we have already seen, the part nearest Victoria Road was known as 'Short Hedge' or 'Edge' after the hawthorn hedges which bounded each side of the road. The road was formerly known as 'Horse Fair', since it was the regular site for this important event.

The *High Street* is first named as such in 1581. It was the setting for an annual hiring fair for farm labourers looking for employment.

Little London was the home of a small migrant population from the capital, sometime at the beginning of the 19th century. It was known as 'Little London Lane' in 1807 and as 'London Street' in 1855. The stretch north of Church Road was referred to separately as 'Back Lane'. Little London boasted Swindon's last remaining thatched cottage until the 1960s. Victory Row, built off the street in 1879, was also demolished in the 1960s.

Newport Street is first recorded in 1346 as 'Nyweport Street', which is thought to mean 'the new market'. It was also sometimes known as 'Bull Street' after the *Bull Inn*: evidently this was a hostelry of ill repute, for Richard Jefferies called it a 'disgrace to the town'.

Wood Street was known as such in the reign of Queen Elizabeth I, when it was named in the lease of a tenement dated 1599. A third of the houses here were still thatched early in this century. There were no buildings on the left-hand side of the road leading towards Wootton Bassett beyond Mr. Chandler's shop.

Swindon remained a very rural community until the cutting of the Wiltshire and Berkshire Canal reached the town in 1805, stimulating trade and development. The canal was intended to link the Kennet and Avon Canal at Semington with the Thames and Severn Canal at Abingdon. The connection was completed in 1810, and a further branch of 8¾ miles to Latton, containing 12 locks, was completed in 1819. The canal had a short life, however; only 30 years after its opening its trade was almost entirely destroyed by the arrival of the Great Western Railway.

Authorisation for the construction of railway workshops at Swindon was given in February 1841, and they were in use by November of the following year. A 'New Swindon' quickly established itself to the north of the old settlement on the hill. Early 'New Swindon' consisted of a development of 300 uniform cottages around a central square. They were designed by Sir Matthew Digby Wyatt, the architect of Paddington Station. The cottages and other village build-

An aerial view painting of New Swindon in 1849, looking east towards London. On the left are the G.W.R. Works and on the right is New Swindon, the railway village built of a combination of local stone and stone made available by the cutting of Box Hill. The houses were small by modern standards but well designed for that period, each with its own toilet, two bedrooms and a small garden. In 1867 Richard Jefferies called New Swindon 'The Chicago of the Western Counties'.

ings were constructed of Bath and Swindon stone, which was brought across Cambria Bridge from the old town. Building work began in 1843, and took 10 years to complete. The square was called 'High Street' (it had no connection with the old High Street in Old Swindon), and all the other streets took their names from towns and cities in the Great Western Railway's empire. Each row of cottages ends at a three-storey building called 'Rigby Cottages', after the original contractors J & C Rigby of Millbank, London.

By the turn of this century, New Swindon had expanded sufficiently to join with the old town and form the Borough of Swindon. Life in the early part of this century is recalled by May Scott, who was born there in 1910. Her son, Christopher L. Scott, introduces his mother's recollections:

'One of the most fascinating aspects of local history, indeed any historical work, is dealing with primary sources, looking at original documents or contemporary biographies. One of the greatest, and under-used, devices of our time is the portable tape-recorder with which an enthusiast can gather information and details by getting people to talk about the past. One of the major resources for local history is right here on our doorsteps, or even in our armchairs, the memories of the senior citizens which are packed with lively anecdotes, nostalgic reminiscences and fine details. Sometimes age does play tricks, dates blend and names alter, but often memories are razor-sharp and true fountains of knowledge. I have requested my mother to put together a collection her thoughts and memories about life here during the early part of the century.'

MAY SCOTT'S MEMORIES

I was born in April 1910 and lived for the first 45 years of my life in Swindon. I still visit the town frequently and can only marvel at the number of great changes that the town has undergone since I left. I am told that the old 'Railway Town' has been replaced by 'New Tech City', and that we lie no longer amid the Marlborough Downs but in 'Silicon Chip Valley' – it is all very strange. Memories of old Swindon are both vivid *and* cloudy, so I hope you will forgive the occasional slip; most of all, I hope you find this useful and enjoyable.

In August 1914 I was four, and we lived in a terraced house in Rodbourne. My first recollction of World War One was seeing my father marching up Rodbourne Road. He was in the front rank of a group of uniformed soldiers, proudly striding out in a navy suit and bowler hat. He had just enlisted! He was with the first Swindonians to go over to France I suppose; I don't recall if mother knew where he was going when he went out, but we never saw him again until he came home from the Front. He brought home with him a box of cream sweets, like fondants, packed in a round box and tied up like a tramp's dinner in a red and white spotted handkerchief. We children were gathering clover for the family's rabbits, destined for the table, when he arrived but my brother wasn't too keen to see him ... his teacher's husband was at the Front too and had promised to tell Dad all the naughty things we had been up to. I had started school at three years old as we all seemed to do then. We all wore white pinafores and thick black stockings and sat in straight lines on hard forms. Often shopping was done on the way home, especially fetching fresh bread from Hawkins' Bakery and eating the crust off the top while walking home ... or even the soft side pieces which didn't show too much. Rationing and shortages seemed to be an everyday thing during the War and walking to Bridge Street to queue at The Maypole for butter was a regular task for us children. We couldn't afford trams, even if they were noisy, busy, exciting rides. It was pleasant to dream about one day riding the trams, or even working on them, as for the first time women were now employed as conductresses while the men were away.

Long hair was the fashion for us girls, long tresses which were ideal for lice! It was no consolation to be told 'clean hair attracted nits' after submitting to the searches of 'Nitty Nora' two or even three times a week, when a small tooth comb was painfully dragged across the head on safari for 'game'. If by chance they found any, 'dirty' children were given notes for their parents explaining how to treat the condition – a liberal dousing with vinegar and paraffin!

Food was naturally short during the '14-'18 War and tea time was a slice of bread with marg. or jam, never both. Biscuits were a luxury, but sometimes we had broken ones from Freeth's or Mrs. May's as a special treat. Mr. Brown the milkman used to come round with his horse-drawn float, and he would ladle out half or full pint measures straight from the churn into bowls or jugs we took out to him. Delivering street traders were the norm then, no persecutions or threats of 'causing a nuisance'. Withers the muffin-man ringing his bell and his flat tray balanced precariously on his head was a traditional feature of Sunday. Bakers too worked off the back of horse carts, and so did salt merchants, ladies with big cotton bonnets and large white pieces falling down the back to keep the salt out of their hair. They sold oblongs of solid salt and dragged them off the carts and into the houses. It was all a far cry from hypermarkets, shopping precincts and cheque-book purchasing of today.

Most of our fathers worked 'inside'; inside the Great Western Works that is, but the G.W.R. had its effect on us 'outside' just as much as on those who actually joined that huge moving river of men every morning. Their carts came round the streets. They dropped off old timber, cracked and broken sleepers soaked in pitch which were avidly sought after for winter fuel. Coal too was supplied at a very low cost and always brought to the door. The company did a great deal for its workers in comparison with other firms of its day. Privilege tickets were available to employees, a system I believe still exists today, and so cheap travel became possible, if you had anywhere to go to. And, although it was a very difficult task, once a boy got an apprenticeship (usually through his dad's influence) he was in for the rest of his working life. Everything seemed to revolve around the works: that's how it seemed to us children outside.

We timed our clocks with the hooters: ten-to-eight, five-to-eight and eight o'clock and we sometimes jeered at the 'late men' as they hurried past for the gates. 'You're gonna be late mister!' 'The hooter's about to go!' Then at 12.30 it went again for lunch break and we knew it was time go home for dinner with the family if dad came home. Then 1.20, 1.25 and 1.30 told the start back sequence, and the final one came at 5.30 telling the workmen to 'knock off', or to tell us out in the fields or playing in the streets that it was time for tea.

The first Friday in July was Trip Day, the bright spot of the year when trains would throng the sidings between Purton Bridge and Rodbourne Bridges and steam away to the seaside; to places like Weston, Weymouth and Teignmouth. It seemed the whole of Swindon was on the move that day. It wasn't of course, free passes weren't for everybody and holidays were lock-outs, so money was tight. You could go for a week if you could afford it but most families tried to get their passes and get down to the sea for a glorious outing. 'Carry your cases for a penny.' 'Which trains for Weymouth.' 'Anyone seen our youngest?' Trip Day was a mad whirl of excitement even before the train actually left. There were grand fetes in the G.W.R. Park. These fetes happened two or three times a year and children whose fathers were members of the Mechanics Institute were given a bag of cakes and a ticket for a free ride on the roundabout, as well as free cups of tea. We were always very glad dad was a member.

The Mechanics was the centre for lots of families. That large gothic building pulsated with life and always had something going on: billiards, snooker and whist for the less active, a band, sports and skittles for the energetic. There was an active theatre in the place, which put on shows to rival the old *Empire*. It even had a library, no browsing though, you chose your book by number, rather like the way people take out videos these days.

One of the real ways the G.W.R. affected the town was through its Medical Fund. Employees were stopped a few pence every week out of their wages which entitled them and their families to treatment and medicines and the services of a doctor employed at the surgery on the corner of Milton and Faringdon Roads which is still there today. There was also a dentist and an optician on the premises and teeth were drawn and dentures fitted on the same day, eyes were tested and glasses fitted free at the same speed. It probably left a lot to be desired in the eyes of modern critics but to us it was marvellous. The Medical Fund was the society on which Bevan based the National Health Scheme, but prevention rather than cure was our mother's doctrine. Every Friday night we were dosed with liquorice powder, got from the Medical Fund, to keep our bowels free – a somewhat puritan regime. It was a recognised thing that we children were sent to Sunday School, both morning and afternoon. With normal family worship at 11.00 and 6.30 we needed the change of alternating round the Wesleyan Chapel, Primitive Methodists, Railway Mission and Salvation Army services!

The streets were our playgrounds, there were no problems with cars. We played with whips and tops, frantically bowled hoops along the pavements, chalked the paving slabs out for hopscotch and played marbles along the gutters. Oranges were delivered to the greengrocers in slatted wooden cases, bound by plaited raffia or grass. These were replaited to make ropes for skipping, tug-o-war or even for tying on the gas-lamp posts to make improvised swings. Sometimes neighbours would insist 'you'll break 'em and then you'll pay', but the cast iron never seemed to move beneath the weight, no matter how many got on the rope. Other neighbours provided sweets, the lady across the road from us produced the largest humbugs you ever saw. Sometimes when we had a ½d we would go up to Nash's sweet shop for a '½d big lot' or collect some mouthwatering 'dandelion and burdock' in a jar from Bounds.

We weren't always good — few children are — sometimes we would go into another street and sprint down the front of the houses knocking on each door, never daring to turn round and see who came out in case they recognised you and told your dad. Some of the boys would arm themselves with pointed stocks, dash past the greengrocers and spear fruit or vegetables, bearing them away in triumph. This merited quite a telling off, or even the stick, and was seldom repeated more than twice in any young boy's adventures.

'Waste not' was a constant watchword. Early on we weren't allowed candles upstairs; they were for the parlour and kitchen only. When gas lamps went into the downstairs room we could have candles in our bedrooms, but only one. But by a couple of small, although aged, mirrors they produced enough light to get undressed or even read by! We had our bath once a week, in the large tin bath in front of the fire for winter or out in the kitchen for summer. The children had to fill the great coppers from the tap and carry the heated water from place to place in buckets. Very few working-class houses had sinks. Mother agreed with frequent washing, especially when the G.W.R. foundry was working and smuts got everywhere. Even walking beneath Rodbourne Bridge we got filthy, and as we walked from the Drill Hall to our street so we crunched along on a layer of gritty soot and left a black cloud behind us.

Growing up in a railway town was never easy, but it was never unbearable. It was hard but you don't seem to notice until you get some of the easier things which modern living has brought us. This brief insight has brought back many memories, but the one thing which impresses me most is the tremendous changes we have seen in our lifetime. People going to the moon was fantasy in those early years, and international video links not even dreamed of. For all its industry and size, the railway town was a much smaller place with a greater sense of community.

* * * * *

It is hoped that the following collection of pictures, illustrating many aspects of Swindon's development between the mid-19th century and the middle of the present century, will bring alive once more the Swindon of the past. Perhaps these pictures will rekindle for old Swindonians the sense of community which May Scott sadly feels has now been lost, and will enable newer residents of Swindon to imagine life in the small railway town they never knew.

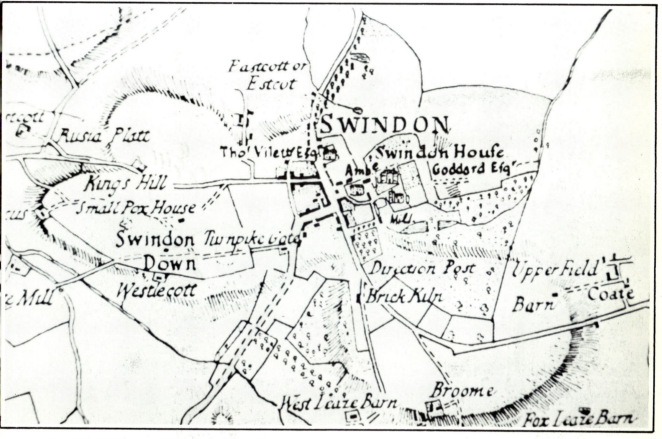

1. This 1773 map of Swindon shows that the town evolved around the four main streets. Swindon had expanded during the previous century partly as a result of the misfortunes of the town of Highworth six miles away. A considerable proportion of Highworth's population transferred to Swindon to escape the plague ravaging the former village. The Small Pox House on the outskirts of the town was the place to which you were sent, in isolation, if you were unfortunate enough to contract the disease.

Churches of Swindon

2.   This drawing of a part of Old Swindon was done by John Luckett Jefferies, a relative of the writer Richard Jefferies, around 1845. He drew this view from the junction of The Planks and Old Mill Lane. In the background is Holy Rood, the original parish church of Swindon and in the foreground stands the town's mill, which stood on a slope down from the Market Square and was driven by water from the town pond; traces of the lip of the dam can still be seen in the lie of the land today. The mill was certainly working in the mid-18th century and the building survived until the 1850s.

3. One of the earliest photographs of Swindon is also of Holy Rood Church, and was taken by Nevil Storey-Maskelyne of Bassett Down House in 1847. He was a friend of W. H. Fox-Talbot who invented negative-positive photography, which he patented in 1842. Holy Rood was first mentioned in written documents in 1154, was in use until the dedication of Christ Church in 1851, and was partly demolished the following year.

4. This view from the south-east shows the chancel of Holy Rood as it was in the early part of the 20th century.

5. This pre-1914 photograph was taken from the rear of the Corn Exchange and shows The Planks, the principal route to Holy Rood. The door to the extreme left led to the vicarage. The vicar and his parishioners had to pass along this lane, through the archway to the church. As a pond lay in front of the church, used by cattle, this path could be a positive quagmire, threatening Sunday-best clothes. Therefore the pathway was raised, originally by planks of wood, which were later replaced by stone.

6. (*opposite below*) The arrival of the railway in Swindon in the 1840s caused a rapid increase in the town's population. People moved up from the New Town to the Old Town and this necessitated the building of a larger church. The foundation stone for Christ Church was laid in 1850 and the church was dedicated the following year. It took from the original parish church of Holy Rood five bells dated 1741, which were re-cast, and the tower clock which dated from 1843. Christ Church was designed by George Gilbert Scott (1811-78) in a late 13th-century style and closely resembled the church of Buchworth in Huntingdonshire. This photograph shows the church in the early 1900s.

7. (*above*) The almshouses, situated to the right of the church, are numbers 27-30 Cricklade Street and were built in 1877. The inscription on the building reads:

'Anderson's Hostel—1877. From a bequest left by the late Mr. Anderson of this town for the second poor of Swindon. The trustees have erected this hostel. They have also invested five hundred pounds to provide an annual endowment and one hundred pounds as a repairing fund for the same.'

The following names are also recorded on the inscription: Henry George Baily (vicar) as a trustee, John Chandler and Robert Smith-Edmonds as church wardens, and George Henry Read as architect.

This photograph dates from 1900.

8. The Bath Road Methodist Church in 1880, soon after its completion. This building replaced an earlier octagonal chapel at the rear of the Corn Exchange.

9. Wesley Chapel, Farringdon Road, 1913. Near the G.W.R. Hospital stood 'The Barracks', a large railway house which was used as a hostel with 100 beds for single men. In 1867 it became a Wesleyan Methodist Chapel and by 1962 it had become Swindon's Railway Museum.

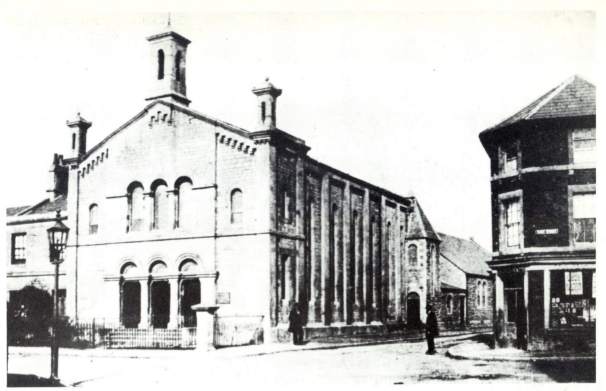

10.   This photograph shows the Baptist Church in 1880. The church was built in 1849 in Fleetway Terrace, a road which follows the path of an ancient walkway known as the Fleetway. The church was replaced by the Baptist tabernacle in Regent Circus in 1886.

11.   Architect's design for the Baptist tabernacle, 1884.

12. (*left*) The Baptist tabernacle, pre-1914.

13. (*below*) Inside the Baptist tabernacle, *c.*1893.

14. (*above*) The Roman Catholic Church, Regent Circus, *c.*1900. This church was opened around 1882 and was used until Holy Rood, Groundwell Road, was built in 1905. The building was opened in 1920 as Swindon's first museum, and as such remained standing for a further ten years before demolition.

15. (*below*) St Mark's Church, built in 1845. The building was designed by George Gilbert Scott, and was funded initially by £500 left in his will by a director of the G.W.R. Works, C. H. Gibbs, towards a church and school. The final cost of the building was £6,000.

The Lawn

The Lawn was originally the home of the Goddard family who were the major landowners in the area. They came to Swindon from a little village called Upper Upham in the Marlborough Downs and had been connected with the town since 1404. Then in 1563 Thomas Goddard bought the old Manor House on its hilltop site. The classical facade dates from the mid-18th century, the house having been extended and altered as family fortunes grew. By 1852 an impressive Italian-style sunken garden had been laid.

By the 1880s the Goddard family included members of parliament and state officials, and marriages with other local dignitaries ensured a powerful hold on local affairs. Like any great house it had its staff of servants who were often recruited locally. They too were often involved in public events and traditionally made and sold ice-cream for charity. This was a popular attraction at the annual Victoria Hospital fete, where the ice-cream was always sold out, people being keen to taste what the gentry ate up on 'Nob Hill'.

However, fortunes changed and the family gradually dispersed; the last lord of the manor, Fitzroy Pleydell Goddard, died in 1927 and his widow four years later. From 1931 the house remained unoccupied and the army of servants and workers gradually melted away. Given a brief respite when American troops were billeted there during World War II, the house eventually deteriorated beyond repair by the late 1940s and, with no family concern and no public investment, this once proud, fine old property was pulled down in 1952.

16. The Lawn, West End Gardens, post 1852.

17. The Lawn viewed from The Planks about 1914.

18. The Lawn, West End Gardens, in the 1920s.

19. (*above*) Ambrose Lethbridge Goddard and his wife, Charlotte, with their family, *c*. 1880. Goddard (1819-98) was lord of the manor of Swindon and lived at The Lawn.

20. (*left*) The last lord of the manor, Fitzroy Pleydell Goddard, and his favourite parrot, *c*. 1921. In 1907 Fitzroy Pleydell had been High Sheriff of Wiltshire.

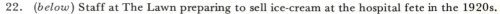

21. (*above*) Housemaids and chambermaids of The Lawn pose in front of the dark trades-men's entrance for a group portrait between chores, sometime in the 1920s.

22. (*below*) Staff at The Lawn preparing to sell ice-cream at the hospital fete in the 1920s.

23. (*above*) The Goddard coach at Salisbury, 1907.

24. (*right*) The Lawn during the heavy snows of Easter 1908.

25. (*below*) The Lawn drive at the same time. This photograph is dated 24 April 1908.

26. The Goddard coachman, Arthur George Millin, in 1907.

Local Buildings

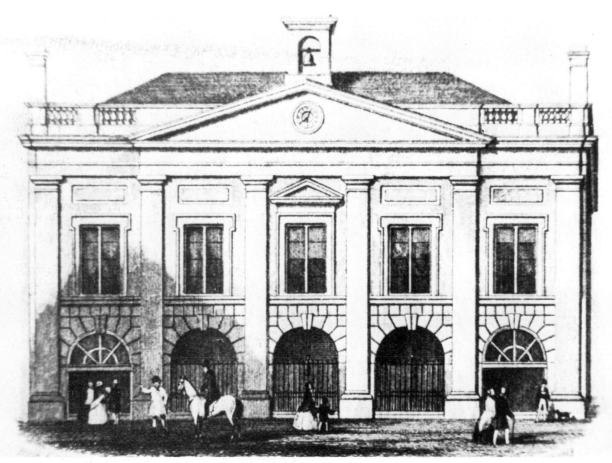

27.   The impressive classical Town Hall was completed in 1852 and although originally designed as a market-house, was used extensively as a meeting place and for magisterial business which transferred there from the *Goddard Arms* in the High Street. This picture was drawn during the year the building was completed.

28. & 29.   The adjacent Corn Exchange was added in 1866 and was officially opened by a sumptuous public dinner at which the building was blessed by an endless succession of toasts. The 80 foot clock has dominated the Swindon skyline ever since. The inscription above the door reads 'Blessed be the Lord who daily loadeth us with benefits'. The Corn Exchange became a centre of the community and hosted carnivals, political rallies and hunt functions. In 1909 it became a roller skating rink. The photograph above (28) was taken in 1900 and the one to the right (29) in February 1923.

30. The view from the clock tower is impressive. In the past the sweeping panorama to be seen included Goddard land across to Liddington Hill, the vicarage and coaching stables, as well as The Lawn. This view from the tower in 1923 shows the market square, with the spire of Christ Church in the distance.

31. The post office, Regent Circus, built in 1900.

32. (*above*) Jefferies Farmhouse at Coate, *c.*1900.
The romantic writer and poet, Richard Jefferies (1848-1887), lived at the farmhouse at Coate, a village two miles south of Swindon, and wrote a great deal of his adventurous childhood in and around the reservoir there.

33. (*right*) Richard Jefferies at 14 years, 1862.

The G.W.R. Hospital opened in 1872 as a cottage hospital for the treatment of members of the G.W.R. Medical Fund which was formed in 1847, and consisted of four beds, operating rooms, bathroom, surgery, mortuary and nurses' home. To the right of the hospital the pair of gates marked the boundary between Railway and common ground. All the gates to the railway estate were closed on one day a year, restricting access to the village. This was a mark of respect for the property of the G.W.R. The gates near the hospital are believed to have been locked every Good Friday.

34. (*above*) G.W.R. Hospital, 1903.

35. (*left*) G.W.R. Hospital, 1910.

36. The interior of the Victoria Hospital during Christmas celebrations.

The Empire Theatre, Swindon

37. Queen's Theatre, built 1897. The building was designed by Drake & Pizey of Bristol and was described by Sir John Betjeman as being in a 'gay Flemish Renaissance' style. At the start of the present century it became the Empire Theatre. The Empire was closed in January 1955 and the building demolished in 1959.

38. Swindon's Electricity Works in Corporation Street. Under the terms of an electric lighting order from the New Swindon Urban District Council, these works were opened in 1903 on a site formerly occupied by Eastcott Farm.

Special Occasions

39. (*left*) The High Street in 1887 on the occasion of Queen Victoria's Golden Jubilee, which provided an excuse to put out miles of bunting and to show off those amazing penny-farthings.

40. (*below*) The Royal Wiltshire Yeomanry returning from South Africa, 9 July 1901. A civic reception was held at the Town Hall.

41. The *Bell Hotel* decorated to celebrate the coronation of George V on 23 June 1911. The stone above the entrance to the *Bell* in the High Street claims that the building dates from 1515, in the reign of King Henry VIII. Unfortunately, this stone is probably the only part of the original building which remains, though it could well have been built in that year. The existing building dates from the mid-19th century. The *Bell*, as well as being the town's post office, was a principal coaching house in Swindon, coaches leaving three times a week for London.

The *Bell* is believed to have taken its name from 'bellarmine', a jar with a narrow neck, a fat belly, and often with a handle at the back, which was almost certainly used to contain ale. Such jars originated in the Low Countries, from where the original builders/occupiers of the building came. Goddard deeds of 1649 state that this building was called the *Lapwing*; however, it was certainly called the *Bell* by 1764.

42. (*left*) The Town Hall at the time of the 1911 coronation celebrations.

43. (*below*) Regent Street on the same occasion.

44. Unveiling the cenotaph, 30 October 1920. The new cenotaph, modelled on Whitehall, replaced a temporary wooden one. Originally, in July 1919, a 50 foot flagpole had been erected on this site as part of the peace celebrations, but during a procession a soldier had publicly criticised the council's expenditure of £200 on this monument, whilst ignoring the plight of ex-servicemen. The speech incited the crowd to take petrol and tar and burn down the offending flagpole, dancing and singing around the fire to express their disgust at the council's parsimony.

45. Swindon's local author, Richard Jefferies, was celebrated in a Jefferies festival which was organised by 400 members of the Workers' Educational Association, who met in the Old Town and walked across the fields to Coate. This photograph shows the unveiling ceremony at the farmhouse (*see* plate 32) on 20 June 1911.

46. Regent Street during the 1911 coronation celebrations.

Visit of Their Majesties the King and Queen
to Swindon, April 28th, 1924.

𝕻rogramme

12-55 p.m.   Departure of Royal Train from Windsor.   Luncheon to be served en route to Swindon.

2-10 p.m.   Arrival at Swindon Station.   Their Majesties will be received by the Lord Lieutenant of the County, the Viscount Long, and Viscountess Long.   The Lord Lieutenant will present :—

> The Mayor and Mayoress of Swindon,
>   (Mr. and Mrs. T. C. Newman).
>
> The Town Clerk (Mr. R. Hilton).
>
> Mr. R. Mitchell Banks, K.C., M.P. for the Swindon Division of Wiltshire.
>
> Mr. C. B. Collett, O.B.E. (Chief Mechanical Engineer, Great Western Railway).

2-15 p.m.   Drive from Swindon Station.   The procession will be formed at the Station :—

> 1st Car—The King and Queen
>   The Lord Lieutenant
>   The Chief Constable (on the box)
>
> 2nd Car—The Lady-in-Waiting
>   Viscountess Long
>   The Mayor
>   Equerry-in-Waiting

47.   The first page of the Programme for the royal visit to Swindon in 1924. The following pages outline events arranged for later in the afternoon: 2.30 p.m. His Majesty was to place a wreath at the cenotaph, after which he and the queen were to proceed to the Town Hall to be received by the Mayor. At 2.45 p.m. they were to inspect a new section of the Victoria Hospital. Then they were to go to the Swindon Works where they would see the G.W.R. Medical Fund Surgery at 3.10 p.m., followed by the Accident Hospital and the Mechanics' Institution. At 3.15 p.m. they were to inspect the Works with Mr. Collett, Chief Mechanical Engineer. At 5.00 p.m. the Royal Train was to depart from Swindon Station, arriving at Windsor Station at 6.15 p.m.

48. The queen with Mr. C. B. Collett, Chief Mechanical Engineer at the Swindon Works 1922-41.

49. (*above*) Crowds at the cenotaph on the occasion of the royal visit in 1924. Their Majesties laid a wreath at the cenotaph.

50. (*below*) The king and queen emerging from the Town Hall in Regent Circus with the Mayor, Alderman T. C. Newman.

51. G.W.R. workers casting a plate of welcome to the royal visitors. This large plate (at least eight feet square) still hangs in the Works today.

52. Their Majesties at the G.W.R. Works.

53. An unscheduled moment in the royal programme was when the king asked to drive the royal train the one mile from the Works to the station. He had a special interest in No. 4082, *Windsor Castle*, and believed he drove this. In fact, however, the *Windsor Castle* was not available at that time so he drove an identical locomotive, complete with new name and number plate, to make it seem to be the train he had requested!

54. May Day celebrations at College Street School, *c.* 1926. The original G.W.R. school was in Bristol Street, but it became overcrowded after boys' and girls' classes were separated in 1869. As a result, the girls moved to The Barracks (Wesley Chapel) in 1871, then to the Drill Hall in the G.W.R. Park in 1872 and finally to College Street in 1874. These premises were erected in 1873 behind the Wilts. & Berks. Canal, which was presumably rather hazardous for the pupils.

Earning A Living

The Town Hall building has been occupied for many years by Brown & Nephew (later Brown & Plummer), Wine Merchants. The cellars were a central feature in the smuggling trade in which Swindon was deeply involved. The steps to the cellars are all tombstones; although well-worn, they can still be distinguished today. Many of the old tunnels that run beneath the town form part of the cellars of this building. These vaults are said to be haunted by the ghost of a 19th-century cellarman and smuggler, Lawrence, who drowned himself in the pond in front of the church to escape the pursuing customs and excise men. Two later cellarmen, Baxter and Hedges, swore that they often saw his ghost.

55. The order office of Brown & Plummer, February 1923. In the top left hand corner is an Anti-Prohibition poster which reads: 'WARNING. Indifference of the Public resulted in America going dry. USE YOUR VOTE AND INFLUENCE AGAINST LOCAL OPTION. It is the thin end of the wedge of prohibition.'.

SWINDON & MARLBOROUGH.

BROWN & PLUMMER,

IMPORTERS OF

FOREIGN WINES & SPIRITS

AGENTS FOR

BASS & CO.'S ALE, GUINNESS & CO.'S STOUTS,
And JAMESON, PIM & CO.'S INVALIDS' STOUTS.

HOP FACTORS.

CHOICE FOREIGN CIGARS.

BONDED WAREHOUSES:

42, Cricklade Street, Swindon.

(Traders desiring to BOND will be Treated with on Liberal Terms)

OFFICES & DUTY PAID CELLARS:

MARKET PLACE, SWINDON.

BRANCHES:

2, Faringdon Street, New Swindon,

AND

HIGH STREET, MARLBOROUGH.

NOTE:—For the convenience of Private Families they are now
delivering Messrs. Bass & Co.'s Burton Ales; Messrs. Guinness
and Son's Dublin Stout, and Messrs. Jameson, Pim & Co.'s
INVALIDS' STOUT, in 9 gallon Casks.

56.   Brown & Plummer trade notice from the 1884 Swindon Directory.

57. (*above*) Bottle washing at Brown & Plummer, February 1923.
58. (*below*) The cellars at Brown & Plummer, February 1923.

59. The storeroom at Brown & Plummer, February 1923.

60. E. Smith's butcher's shop, c.1910. Formerly this was the *King of Prussia* public house, which on fair days gained a great deal of custom, from the assembly room at the rear. Music was provided by the violin of a travelling gypsy whose repertoire was limited to one tune! The *King of Prussia* was owned for some time by the notorious 'Fat Billy Webb' and it was reported that he was so large that he had great difficulty even getting through the door! The inn of ill-repute was closed in 1880 when the butcher Smith moved in. The building remained butcher's premises until shortly before it was demolished in 1981.

61.   This photograph was taken soon after the opening of the Wiltshire & Dorset Bank on Thursday 5 February 1885. The bank stands on the corner of Wood Street and Cricklade Street. It was by no means Swindon's first bank, which was opened in the first decade of the 19th century by Messrs. Strange, Garrett, Strange & Cook (later James and Richard Strange), and was taken over by the County of Gloucester Banking Company in 1842.

The site of the Wilts. & Dorset Bank was formerly the premises of another butcher's—Blackford. Robert Blackford was a local champion in the game of backswording.

The large man on the left of the photograph is William Morris who lived at what are today the offices of the *Evening Advertiser*, the local paper which he founded in 1854. Limmex hardware store, which was established in the 1870s, has been trading in these premises near the bank for well over a century, the buildings dating from *c.*1705.

The CORNER SHOP

(OPPOSITE THE GODDARD ARMS HOTEL,)

HIGH STREET, SWINDON.

S. J. LIMMEX,

Begs to solicit your patronage to the above address, where a good selection of

IRONMONGERY

Of almost every description is kept in Stock, comprising

BEST SHEFFIELD CUTLERY, SCISSORS, &c. ELECTRO-PLATED AND BRITANNIA METAL GOODS, TEA & COFFEE POTS, CRUET FRAMES, SPOONS, FORKS, GRAVY SPOONS, SAUCE LADLES, TOAST RACKS, &c.

FENDERS, FIRE-IRONS, COAL VASES, TEA TRAYS, &c.

SAUCEPANS, POTS, KETTLES, FRYING PANS, ENAMELLED GOODS, TIN WARE of all Sorts.

BATHS, TOILET SETS, HOT-WATER CANS, HOT-WATER BOTTLES

BRUSHES, BROOMS, MATS, MOPS, SPONGES, CHAMOIS LEATHERS

A GREAT VARIETY OF

LAMPS.

Lamp Oils, Machinery Oils, Linseed Oil, Turpentine, Petroleum, Benzoline, Naptha.

PAINTS, COLOURS, AND VARNISHES

62.   Limmex trade notice from the 1884 Swindon Directory.

KITCHEN RANGES, GRATES, &c.

THE PRIZE KITCHENER

Closed & Open Fire Kitchen Grates, Register Stoves, Shop Stoves, Paraffin Stoves, Gas Stoves, &c., kept in Stock to select from.

Any Pattern not on hand immediately procured on application.

DAIRY REQUISITES:

Stamped Milk Pans, Milk Buckets, Cream Tins, Cheese Tubs, Milk Warmers, Milk Coolers, Skimmers, Curd Mills, Curd Breakers, Curd Knives, Barrel Churns, Butter Prints, Butter Rolls, Scotch Hands, &c.

Any Article made on the Premises of any required Shape or Size.

Hot Water Apparatus for Cheese Rooms, Attemporators, &c., Fixed on the most approved principles, to order.

Special attention is given to the selection of the

CARPENTERS' TOOLS

Kept in Stock.   All best Tools are Warranted, and Exchanged at once if not satisfactory.

S. J. LIMMEX,

THE CORNER SHOP,

HIGH STREET, SWINDON,

(OPPOSITE THE GODDARD ARMS HOTEL.)

63. Built after 1782, the *Goddard Arms Hotel* replaced an earlier thatched building known as the *Crown*, which was certainly in existence by 1621. The *Crown* was one of the infamous nine alehouses reputed to be 'too many' for a town of barely 300 inhabitants, according to the report of 1627 by the constables of Kingsbridge Hundred. Magistrates' sessions were held there until they were transferred to the new Town Hall shortly after it was opened in 1852. This photograph shows the *Goddard Arms* in the early 1900s.

64. This very early photograph of Cricklade Street, which has retained this name since at least 1663, was taken before 1884 and shows the premises of Isaac Ann, printers and publishers.

THE CELEBRATED

WARMINSTER ALES.

JAMES BARTLETT & SONS,

High Street Brewery,

WARMINSTER,

In acknowledging the increased Patronage accorded to their Ales by the Public of Swindon and District, beg to assure them that it is their endeavour, by maintaining the high standard of quality, to merit a still further increase of their support.

SOLE AGENT FOR SWINDON,

Mr. A. W. Deacon,

CORN MERCHANT,

Market Square, OLD SWINDON.

65. Trade notice advertising Warminster Ales, from the 1884 Swindon Directory.

66. (*above*) Shawyer's chemist shop in Wood Street, *c.*1900.
67. (*below*) Shawyer's trade card.

JOHN J. SHAWYER, Established 1818.

Chemist by Examination,

12, Wood St., and 22, Faringdon St., SWINDON, Wilts.

Dauntsey, Chippenham,

ear Sir,

Please send me a box of your Pills. I am suffering from Indigestion
d Giddiness. I was suffering in the same way 2 or 3 years ago, and then
nt for a box of your Pills which restored me to perfect health in a short time.
I may add I am 53, and about 16 stone, and am always hearty, with the
ception of this attack, but anticipate a certain cure from your Pills.

I am, Sir, Yours sincerely, F.S.

S. Take Shawyer's Vegetable Pills for Indigestion, Liver trouble,
Biliousness, Giddiness, Flatulence. Headache, & Stomach troubles.

Note, these Celebrated Pills are Silver Coated. 1/1½ & 2/9 a Box.

68.   Shawyer's trade notice from the 1884 Swindon Directory.

69. & 70. William Hooper (1860-1956) outside his photographic studio at No. 6 Cromwell Street. Hooper had originally been a gamekeeper near Gloucester but had an argument with the head keeper and joined the G.W.R. at Swindon around the turn of the century. The photograph above was taken *c.*1905 and the one below, which also shows Hooper's assistant, was taken in 1912.

71. Gillings Dairy in County Road. This was owned by the Mr. Gillings who later lived at 'Fairholme', the canal manager's house.

72. Swindon's fire brigade, Cromwell Street, *c.*1922.

73. (*above*) Stroud, the carriage builders.

74. (*left*) This photograph of 1910 shows J. B. Brind, a local farrier in Lower Town, seen here in the entrance to the forge with his daughter and holding a horseshoe. By the time Mr. Brind was called to serve in the Great War he had left this forge for Wroughton, but these premises remained a forge until at least 1935.

75. & 76.   Two photographs of men leaving the G.W.R. Works in Swindon, *c.*1910. The photograph below shows a wave of men emerging from the Rodbourne Lane entrance to the Works, with a tram about to pass under the bridges—not the time to want to go in the opposite direction!

77. Men posing for their photograph at the tunnel entrance outside the G.W.R. Works in 1912.

78. (*above*) Tunley's, Arts and Graphics, have only recently moved from these premises at 14 Gloucester Street. This photograph was taken *c*. 1890.

79. (*below*) Mr. Thomas, milliner of 41 Bridge Street, seems to be benefiting from the free publicity provided by the boy carrying the hat box, seen more clearly in the close up view of part of plate 78.

80. (*above*) Nibblett's, Aerated Water Manufacturer, was founded in Cheltenham in 1845 and by the 1889s had opened a branch in Swindon. They sold lemonade and ginger beer, and moved to Lagos Street in 1902, but by 1910 had sadly ceased trading. This photograph shows a general view of Milford Street in 1890.

81. (*right*) This close up of the above photograph concentrates on the boys congregated outside Nibblett's.

82. (*above*) This 1920s photograph shows Ralph Adams' fishmonger's stall in the covered market.

83. (*below*) Lott & Sons were well-established and well-known ironmongers in Regent Street until the 1960s.

Street Scenes

84. Wood Street, c.1900, showing the bootseller, Cash & Co., which replaced Edward King's bicycle factory. Otherwise Wood Street has changed little over the years. The tall chimneys of the *King's Arms Hotel* mark the site of the windmill which once gave its name to the street. This peaceful scene hardly recalls the turbulent history of the street, for on more than one occasion the local yeomanry charged on horseback, sabres flashing, down its length to disperse riots, demonstrations and even crowds of drunken navvies.

85. A later view down Wood Street into Victoria Street, pre-1914, shows the advance of 1900s technology. The horse and carts have been replaced by cars and lorries, ornate electric lights span the road, and tram lines now trace around the Old Town, linking it with New Town by the precarious steep drop down Victoria Hill away to the left.

A VIEW IN OLD SWINDON

86. Little London was, despite its rural appearance, the slum area of the town and the location for a doss house. This was an area inhabited by large numbers of Londoners. This photograph was taken *c.*1912 by the son of William Morris, Samuel, and it shows the steps coming from the back of the *Rising Sun* public house in Albert Street, known by locals as 'the Roaring Donkey'. Little London boasted the last thatched cottage in Swindon, which remained standing until the 1960s.

87. This photograph of Newport Street in 1910 bears little resemblance to the area today. This street of ancient whitewashed cottages, some of which dated back to 1346, provided homes for the town's lesser tradesmen. These cottages survived until the early 1960s. The *Bull*, a public house which at one time gave its name to the street, stood half way down on the right and was renamed in 1881 after the arrival of the Swindon, Marlborough and Andover Railway.

BATH Rᴅ SWINDON.

88.   Bath Road, c.1900, with the Methodist Church on the right.

89.   Although dated c.1910, this photograph of Lower Town is believed to be of the crowds coming and going to the Bath and West Show, which in 1906 was held at Broome Farm, south of the town. Some of the people who boarded a crowded tram in Market Square were never to get home: it careered down Victoria Hill and crashed on the turn at the bottom. The scene shown on this photograph is late afternoon, about the time the ill-fated tram moved off from beneath the tower in the top right corner. The gentleman driving the second trap was Mr. Rimes, the butcher of No. 1 Wood Street, whose family later ran the town's coach firm and whose name is still emblazoned on modern luxury coaches crossing the continent.

90. (*left*) Bridge Street from Regent Street, 1910.

91. (*below*) Bridge Street in 1890.

92. & 93.   The Golden Lion has a special place in the heart of many Swindonians, for he was the well-loved animal portrayed on the inn sign of the public house (*c.*1845) which gave its name to the bridge linking Bridge Street and Regent Street. Originally a simple wooden construction, Richard Jefferies in 1867 called this bridge a disgrace, and it was replaced three years later by a new iron bridge which was built by the G.W.R. In 1877 a footbridge was added by public subscription as men were often late for work when the bridge was up. This curious and unique bridge was demolished in 1918 as part of the improvements to the tramway system. These two photographs both show the Golden Lion Bridge in about 1900.

94. This photograph shows the market in 1903 at which time work was in progress to cover it. A market had existed on this site since 1892 when it moved from a site directly behind the Mechanics' Institution. The new covered market building remained standing until the mid-1970s.

95.   Floods in Cromwell Street pre-1914.

96.   The tram centre at the junction of Fleet Street and Bridge Street in the 1920s. This area was the terminus for Swindon's tramway system. This photograph shows the view down Fleet Street (once the ancient track known as Fleetway), looking towards Milford Street bridge. On the right of the picture is the *Volunteer Commercial Hotel.*

97.   Regent Street, *c.*1913.

98. Regent Street in 1913.

99.   Cromwell Street in 1913.

100. (*above*) Regent Circus at the start of the present century.

101. (*below*) Milton Road in the snow, 25 April 1908.

DROVE ROAD, SWINDON.

102. (*above*) Drove Road in summer 1905.
103. (*below*) Drove Road in the snows of 1908.

Leisure and Pleasure

104. (*above*) Skating at the Rink, 1911.
105. (*below*) Children's carnival at the Rink, January 1911.

TOWN GARDENS, SWINDON.

106. The Town Gardens were constructed in the worked-out quarries which first gave Swindon its wealth. Since Roman times Purbeck limestone had been quarried here and much of it was ferried up to London to repave the city after the Great Fire in 1666. This local stone was used in many of the cottages and buildings of the Old Town including the Corn Exchange. By 1885 the best stone had gone and the ugly scars were smoothed over with large quantities of topsoil. Gardens were laid out with trees, shrubs and flowers, on several levels linked by a maze of walkways and bridges. The rustic atmosphere of this photograph of the gardens in about 1900 captures the period's preoccupation with an idyllic past. The Town Gardens became an Old Town country haven for the people of the newly-industrialised Swindon. Nannies, promenading couples and reminiscing old folk strolled and sat among the arches, statues and ponds.

The recreation site of Coate Water is really a reservoir built in 1822 as a feeder for the northern branch of the Wilts. & Berks. canal which followed a steady down-hill path through the town. The reservoir was formed by damming a stream which rises in the village of Chiseldon and eventually becomes the River Cole. Eighty acres of woodland were acquired in the area by the council in 1914 for development as a pleasure spot.

The pleasures of boating were enjoyed by all during the early years of this century and special events, regattas and races were organised on public holidays. The still waters of the southern end were far enough away for a quiet row or a private assignation. During many hard winters Coate Water froze over and many budding ice-skaters took advantage of this. Swimming, diving and water polo were also very popular, with local competitions being transferred here from Lechlade Bridge over the Thames. However, there was a danger of weed and deep mud, which together with the polio scare eventually caused the closure of the reservoir as a swimming venue, though boating is still popular even today.

107.   The wooden diving stage at Coate Water in the 1920s.

108. (*right*) The original outlet of the Coate Water reservoir.

109. (*below*) The rear (southern end) of Coate Water reservoir in 1908.

The Mechanics' Institution was established with a view to 'disseminating useful knowledge and encouraging rational amusement' in 1844. Members administered a library which started with 150 books and by 1907 had grown to 10,176. Originally housed inside the factory, the Mechanics' Institution was erected in 1855 by the G.W.R. in the High Street, later renamed Emlyn Square after Lord Emlyn, a former chairman of the Great Western, and leased to members at a nominal rent. The building offered facilities for billiards, cards, lectures on horticulture and art, as well as concerts and plays.

110. The Mechanics' Institution photographed between 1905 and 1914.

111. (*above*) The reading room at the Mechanics' Institution.
112. (*below*) The playhouse theatre at the Mechanics' Institution.

113. The Octagonal Market stood behind the Institution and was opened in 1854, primarily for the benefit of the employees of the G.W.R. Built by Edward Streeter from Bath, it consisted of eight sides each 40 feet long. It was demolished in 1892 when the Mechanics' Institution was extended. It included a beerhouse called the *Engineers' Arms*; off sales were made through a hatch and this gave the building its nick-name of 'The Hole in the Wall'. This photograph shows the Octagonal Market pre-1892.

SWINDON TOWN FOOTBALL CLUB
1946-47.

Mills. Woodman. Saunders. Burton. Boulton. Sturgess. Onslow. Trim. Young.

y Martin. Cousins. Ithell. Parkhouse. Bingham. Lloyd. Lovesey. Emery. Painter. Bert Dav

s Page. Stephens. Denyer. Jones. Stephens. W. Lucas. H. Lucas. Derrick. Edwards. Williams. E. B

114. Swindon Town Football Club was founded by W. B. Pitt in 1881, but struggled to survive until Sam Allen was appointed Manager in 1902. The club's fortunes then took a turn for the better; it won the Dubonnet Cup (Paris) in 1908, the Southern League in 1911 and 1914, and three of its players, Fleming, Walker and Silto, were chosen to play in the England v. Scotland International in 1913. The club's greatest moment of glory was the defeat of Arsenal 3-1, leading to victory in the League Cup in 1969.

115. (*above*) The G.W.R. Park, *c.*1893.

116. (*below*) Cake cutting in the Drill Hall (*see* overleaf for explanation).

The G.W.R. Park played host to the annual Children's Fete for the children of the employees of the Railway. Each child received a slab of fruit cake which had been baked in the Henry Street bakery, a cup of tea, and one free ride on the round-abouts. The backs of their hands were stamped with ink to stop them from trying to re-enter the park for a second piece of cake.

117.   The children's fete in 1919 or 1920.

118. Detail of children at the fete.

119. (*above*) Swindon's first cinema, the
County Electric Pavilion, was opened in
Regent Street on 11 February 1910 by the
Mayor, W. H. Lawson, and members of the
town council. This photograph was taken
soon after the opening ceremony.

120. (*right*) The Picture House was opened
in Regent Circus in 1913. The building later
became a bus waiting room and a boot shop.
The site adjacent to the Picture House
housed the Regent by 1930.

Travel and Transport

121. The *Spotted Cow* on the Coate Road was a popular place for refreshment, perhaps on these 'twopenny-farthing' bicycles. This photograph dates from before 1880.

122. Swindon Junction Railway Station was opened on 14 July 1842. This photograph shows the G.W.R. station in 1912.

123. George Jackson Churchward, C.B.E., who was Chief Mechanical Engineer at the G.W.R.
Works from 1902 until 1921. He was Swindon's first 'Charter Mayor' and was also responsible
for the building of 'City' and 'County' class locomotives. The most famous of these was the
City of Truro which was the first to draw a train at more than 100 m.p.h., a fact not made
known at that time for fear of public reaction against such high speeds. This record was held
from 1903 to 1935.

Swindon is justly proud of its railway heritage and its connection with the Great Western Railway. But there was another company which ran the 'Old Town Line'. The interloper started life as the Swindon, Marlborough and Andover Railway, which tried unsuccessfully to tunnel under Swindon Hill before taking the route around the west side of the town to connect with the G.W.R. main line. The track from Swindon to Marlborough opened in 1881, and that to Andover two years later. With a station off Newport Street, it carried the majority of the town's trade southwards.

Another company was formed to carry the line northwards towards Cheltenham. This merged with the original to form the Midland and South-Western Junction Railway in 1884 (*see* plate 125 opposite), but it was not until 1891 that the M.S.W.J.R. trains finally ran into Cheltenham, by which time the new company's finances were in such a perilous state that it was put into the hands of the receiver.

The great years of the line were in the decade up to World War I when express trains ran between Cheltenham and the south, and the important military link with Tidworth and Salisbury Plain was in constant use.

124. Swindon Town (M.S.W.J.R.) Station in 1881.

M & S.W. Junction Station, Swindon

125. (*above*) The Midland and South-Western Junction Railway.

126. (*below*) Ticket poster from the Midland and South-Western Junction Railway.

127. (*above*) The barrow crossing just west of the station gave an opportunity to move things safely across the line.

128. (*below*) The seemingly ordinary rails in the close up view of plate 127 show Brunel's broad gauge track with a third rail in between so that standard gauge locomotives could run over the same lines.

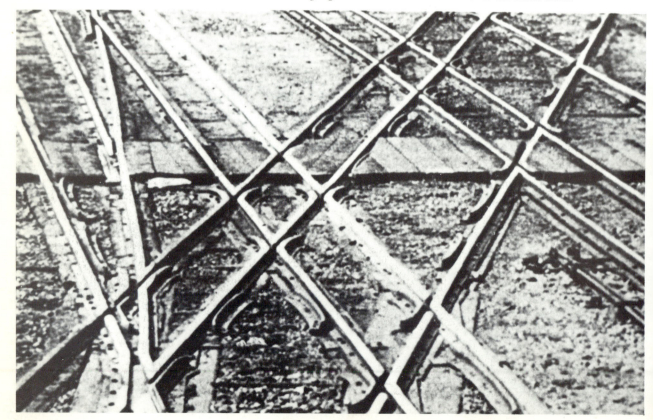

129. The original swimming baths were opened in 1869 next to the canal. F. Large recalls that the '. . . bath tapered from 3ft. 6in. to 7ft.', was 'brick built, cement covered—a dull and drab affair, yet a boon to the Town . . .'.

130. This photograph shows men of the Wilts. Battery and Ammunition column of the 3rd Wessex Brigade of the Royal Field Artillery arriving at Swindon Town Station on 5 August 1914 en route to India. Col. Bedford-Pim and Major the Earl of Suffolk were received by Alderman C. Hill, the Mayor, and members of the council during an official function. Swindon became a frequent last stop for troops destined for the open wilds of Wiltshire.

The origins of the annual trip lay in a privileged offer to members of the Mechanics' Institution of a day excursion to Oxford. The first was in the summer of 1849 when 500 people travelled on a special train. In 1913 the unpaid holiday was extended from a day excursion to a whole week! By 1939 30 special free trip trains were needed to carry the 27,000 people taking advantage of the scheme. Some of the trains were marshalled in sidings and had to be reached through the factory entrances. This was a common trip practice and meant that those who were not lucky enough to find a pair of steps, were obliged to scramble up into the carriages from ground level!

131. A cartoon card, depicting the mad scramble to climb into the 'trip' train.

132. (*above*) The trip in 1910 or 1911.
133. (*below*) The trip in 1912.

134. The trip in 1910.

135. The bridge, shown here in 1912, connected York Road and Graham Street.
This view from the bridge shows the 'ice breaker' slowly rotting; this iron-
bottomed boat was used locally to break ice, often by inviting the local children
to rock the boat to and fro by jumping from one side to the other.

136. & 137. These contrasting pictures, looking towards the Golden Lion Bridge, show the Wilts. & Berks. Canal as it was in about 1908 (above) and as an artist felt it could be (below). By the early years of this century it is obvious that the trade the canal once encouraged had now moved to the Great Western Railway.

Regent Street, Canal and Promenade, Swindon.
(As it might be.)

138. This photograph taken about 1912 shows a well and truly disused canal at the rear of the houses in Medgbury Road. In better days the hoist of Skurray's Mill would have lifted much of the corn used at the mill from the barges on the canal below.

139. Gillings Wharf looking towards the bridge. The Drove Road Wharf was originally called Dunsford Wharf after the first manager, William Dunsford, who lived in the adjacent manager's house from 1817 to 1839. Later the Gillings family, dairy owners and merchants, moved to the house which was sold in 1936 and demolished the following year.

140.   At the end of the North Wilts. branch the canal leaves Swindon through one of the many locks, this one beneath the Telford Road bridge, which was erected between 1814 and 1819 and demolished in the early 1920s. This photograph was taken in 1912.

141.   Cromwell Street Wharf in 1896. In this year the canal had to be blocked in order to lay the foundations of the Central Club and Institute.

WILTS AND BERKS

Canal Carrying Company, Limited,

GENERAL

CARRIERS

Of Merchandise and Goods of all kinds.

WHARVES AT

BRISTOL	DAUNTSEY	LONGCOT
BATH	WOOTTON BASSETT	CHALLOW
BRADFORD	HAY LANE	WANTAGE
MELKSHAM	WROUGHTON	ABINGDON
LACOCK	SWINDON	CRICKLADE
CHIPPENHAM	STRATTON	STROUD AND
CALNE	BOURTON	GLOUCESTER
FOXHAM	UFFINGTON	

ALSO, LANDINGS AT OTHER PLACES.

FREIGHTS CARRIED IN COMPANY'S BOATS,

Which run regularly between Swindon and Bristol; and elsewhere as required.

Through Rates Quoted for Full Loads.

IN COMMUNICATION WITH ALL PARTS.—RATES ON APPLICATION.

BRISTOL DEPOT AND WAREHOUSES,

COUNTERSLIP.

Best Forest, Somerset, and Smith's Coal, Foundry Coke and Small Coal,

GARDEN GRAVEL & ROAD MATERIALS

ALWAYS IN STOCK.

Goods of all descriptions Carried at Moderate Rates.

For Dates of Company's Boats between the above places, carrying less than full loads, and for freights, general information and full particulars, apply to

Mr. FREDERICK HODGES, Manager.

Canal Office, Swindon.

142. Trade notice of the Wilts. & Berks. Canal Carrying Company from the 1884 Swindon Directory.

First Boy: —Hi Bill what be they digging up the road for like that,
Second Boy: —Casnt see ! they be buryin the Hidden Treasure—(Ratepayers' Money)

143. Tram cartoon, 1903.

144. This photograph was taken on 22 September 1904 and shows the opening of the new electric tramway system by the Mayor, J. Hinton. This naturally aroused great public curiosity.

145. A typical tram scene in Regent Circus.

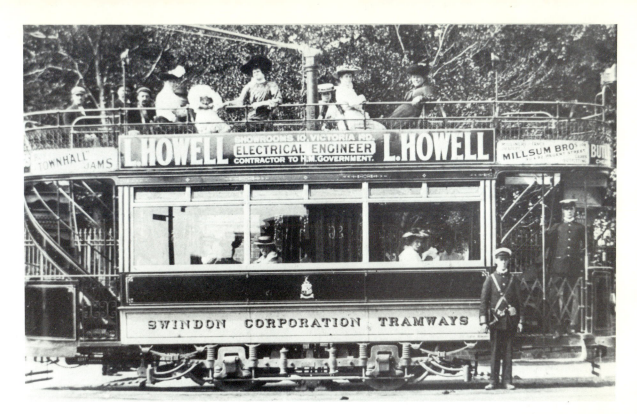

146. (*above*) Ladies in a tram outside the Park in 1906.

147. (*right*) The conductor and driver of the above tram.

148. A tram at the Tram Centre in Fleet Street in 1912.

I Plead for the "TITANIC" Sufferers.

149. (*opposite below*) & 150. (*above*) Bruce was a famous canine charac-
ter, a familiar sight in Swindon between 1905 and 1914. He travelled over
10,000 miles by foot and train, a collecting box strapped to his back. He
collected almost £500 and barked a 'thank you' for each coin. Much of his
work was connected with the Victoria Hospital. He wore a solid silver
collar and was presented with 16 gold and silver medals for his services.
His owner, presumably seen in plate 149, was Mr. T. A. Beal of Nelson
Street in Swindon.

BIBLIOGRAPHY

Backhouse, David W., *Home Brewed*.

Carter, E. R., *History of Bath Road Methodist church*.

Crittall, E. (ed.), *The Victoria County History: Wiltshire*, vol. IX (1970).

Dalby, L. J., *The Swindon Tramways* (1970).

Grinsell, L. V., Wells, H. B., Tallamy, H. S. and Betjeman, John, *Studies in the History of Swindon*.

Large, Frederick, *A Swindon Retrospect*.

Peck, Alan, *The Great Western Railway at Swindon Works* (1983).

Sheldon, Peter, *A Swindon Album*.

Sheldon, Peter and Tomkins, Richard, *Roadways: The History of Swindon's Street Names* (1979).

Silto, J., *A Railway Town*.

Silto, J., *A Swindon History*.